Bristol Radical Pamp

City of Sanctuary?

Seeking refuge in Bristol

Colin Thomas

ISBN 978-1-911522-78-2

Bristol Radical History Group. 2024.
www.brh.org.uk
brh@brh.org.uk

On the Saturday evening of 3rd August 2024, refugees in the Mercure hotel in Bristol heard the menacing sound of a mob approaching. Refugee children were moved to the back of the hotel in the hope that they would be out of earshot of the chants of "Send them back". Anti-fascist demonstrators, aware that hotels housing refugees and asylum seekers were under attack in other UK cities, formed a defensive line outside the Mercure.

According to *Bristol Post* reporter Tristan Cork, "the counter protestors gathered themselves and lined up in front of the main entrance, physically protecting it. They were abused, punched and kicked at." Eventually the police arrived but, as Tristan Cork goes on to stress, the hotel attack "didn't happen, not because the police stopped them, but because ordinary people from Bristol stopped them. They put their bodies on the line, they put themselves in the face of people intent on violence and stood firm".[1] Belatedly the police formed a line of defence and arrested some of those attacking the hotel. A report in *Freedom News* on 6th August recalled "refugees thanking us through the windows of their rooms. They were overjoyed—children and parents were waving and smiling and making hearts out of their hands to us."

Four days later, far right groups threatened to attack the West Street office of a solicitor who helps refugee and asylum seekers, and its windows were boarded up. Thousands of counter-protestors turned up chanting "Whose Streets? Our Streets!", "We are many, You are few, We are Bristol, Who Are You?" and "Say it loud, say it clear, refugees are welcome here." There was no sign of the far right this time.

The events of the first week of August 2024 follow a pattern that stretches back centuries—refugees and asylum seekers seeking refuge in Bristol and encountering hostility from some but a welcome from others. This pamphlet will focus on those who arrived in the city fleeing from persecution rather than those who came to the city primarily to find a better life for themselves and their families.

"The great noise and croaking of the Froglanders"[2]—that's how Sir John Knight, MP for Bristol in 1693, expressed his indignation about the presence of one group of immigrants in in the city. He was just as hostile to Quakers and other religious minorities. His new targets were the Huguenots. The Huguenots were escaping from France because of persecution by King Louis XIV, the Sun King. French Protestants like the

1 Tristan Cork *Bristol Post* 5 August 2024.
2 Quoted in *The Huguenots in Bristol* by Ronald Mayo, Bristol Branch of the Historical Association Reprint 2002, p1.

Huguenots would have had grim memories of the Saint Bartholomew's Day massacre of 1572, "an assault so vicious and terrifying that they had little choice but to flee for their lives".[3] The Edict of Nantes had attempted to reconcile French Protestants to the Catholic State, but Louis XIV had revoked the Edict; Protestant chapels were demolished, their pastors sent as prisoners to row the French galleons; every child was to be brought up Catholic and no Protestant was allowed to leave France.

To escape the dragoons, jackbooted French cavalry men who enforced the new rules, hundreds of Huguenots headed for the French ports and thence to Britain. An attempt was made in Parliament to confer a collective British nationality on all Protestant refugees from the Continent. But Sir John was having none of it. He proposed that Parliament's Sergeant at Arms "be commanded to open the doors and let us first kick the Bill out of the House and then the foreigners out of the Kingdom".[4]

He was outvoted and many Huguenots began the dangerous journey out of France. Daniel Bonnet and his wife hid their two small children in the panniers on a donkey, covered them with vegetables and headed for Bristol. En route in France, they were stopped by a dragoon who demanded to know what was in the panniers. 'Fresh vegetable for the market' the mother replied. The dragoon thrust his sword into the pannier and rode on shouting "Bon voyage mon amis." Once he had gone, the parents opened the pannier to find that, although the child had been wounded in the calf, he had managed to stay silent.[5]

Some of the Huguenots who reached Bristol camped out in St James's churchyard and others outside Lawford's Gate. Local Quakers visited them and distributed relief, recording the case of "James Blondeau a sickly man [and] his wife with a little daughter", and that of Peter Lucas "in great want, being not able to get enough to maintain his family."[6] The Bristol Mayor complained to central government: "The great number and their poverty renders us utterly at a loss how to dispose of them, having more of our own people than we can keep at work with our public stocks".[7]

3 Robert Winder *Bloody Foreigners* Abacus 2014, p63.
4 Quoted by Mayo, op cit, p1.
5 Quoted by Mayo, op cit, p2.
6 Quoted by Madge Dresser and Peter Fleming in *Bristol ethnic minorities and the city 1000-2001* Phillimore 2007, p52.
7 Quoted by Mayo, op cit, p9.

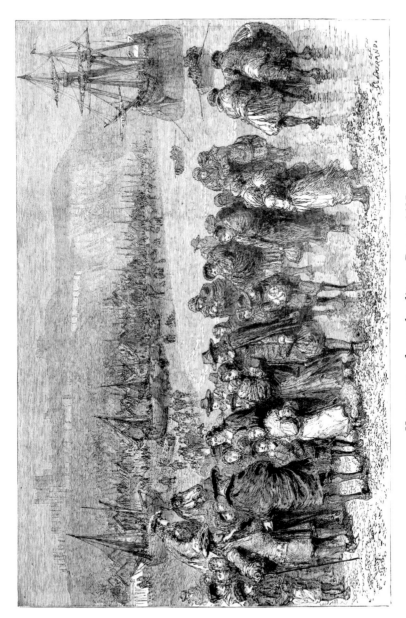

Huguenot refugees landing at Dover, 1685.

Local bishops took a more sympathetic approach. Bishop Ken of Bath and Wells wrote to his clergy urging them to "stir up all under your care to contribute freely and cheerfully to the relief of these distressed Christians", and the Bishop of Bristol offered St Mark's church, the Lord Mayor's chapel, to the Huguenots for their French language services.[8] One estimate suggests that, from the end of the seventeenth century, between 400 and 500 Huguenots moved to Bristol, making up 2.5 per cent of the population.[9]

Sociologist Max Weber, writing at the beginning of the twentieth century, argued that Protestantism was especially congenial to Capitalism, and some of the Huguenots who managed to arrive with funds were able to climb the social ladder in Bristol. Stephen Peloquin traded in tobacco with other Peloquins in America and became a freeman of Bristol. But he refused to take the required oath and so remained outside the tightly-knit Merchant Venturers circle.[10] Ronald Mayo's pamphlet on the Huguenots in Bristol is sympathetic to them but nevertheless says that "their resistance to assimilation by the local population had been expressed from the start by their refusal to abandon their mother tongue and their determination to meet as often as possible to worship and converse in their own language".[11]

Sadly, one Huguenot descendant, James Larouche, did assimilate all too enthusiastically—he became the Sheriff of Bristol from 1764-5 and, as an MP, "primarily represented Bristol's slavery interests, defending the city's stand for free trade in slaves".[12]

Jews in Bristol

European Jews had to wrestle with the same kind of issue that faced the Huguenots in Bristol—assimilation or self-ghettoization. In 1290 all Jews had been expelled from Britain, which was described by Robert Winder, in his book *Bloody Foreigners*, as "both a tragedy and a national disgrace".[13] Unable to return to what some saw as their homeland in Palestine, many Jews settled in Poland, Ukraine and Russia where, whenever there was a crisis, they became readily identifiable scapegoats. They were banned from landownership and Christian craft guilds for

8   Mayo, op cit, p11.
9   Jane Marchese Robinson *Seeking Sanctuary* Pen and Sword History 2020, p15
10 Dresser and Fleming, op cit, p55.
11 Mayo, op cit, p17/18,
12 Mark Steeds and Roger Ball *From Wulfstan to Colston* Bristol Radical History Group 2020.
13 Winder, op cit, p50.

Jacobs Well in Bristol (top-right)—possibly the location of a Jewish ritual bath dating to before 1142.

much of their time in the European diaspora, so Jews had traditionally turned their energies to trade.[14]

In the 1650s, Cromwell encouraged Jews to return to Britain, and Sephardic Jews, intimidated in Spain and Portugal, came, followed, in the 1670s, by Ashkenazi Jews facing similar hostility in Poland and Russia. By 1752 there was a synagogue and burial ground in Bristol, but in that year an Aliens Act to facilitate the naturalisation of Jews in Britain met with vehement opposition. "In November 1752 the Merchants Society unanimously resolved to address the MPs for the city, requesting their aid in procuring the repeal of an Act passed during the previous session permitting English-born Jews to enjoy the privileges of British citizens".[15] Their pressure, and that of the Steadfast Society, led to the almost immediate repeal of the Act.

Even a century later, the *Bristol Times* and *Bristol Mercury*, on 16th July 1853, were still able to claim that "the Jews of Bristol had the unenviable notoriety of being pre-eminent in their unwillingness to listen to the word of God, elsewhere success was more marked." The attitude of the *Bristol Mercury* was a tad more sympathetic: when the Jewess Gertrude Issacs married a Mr Taylor, the newspaper wrote, "We long since admitted the once despised and persecuted Jew to the rights of citizenship, but a few months have passed since the heaviest act of proscription—that which excluded him from his share in the great council of the nation—was swept away by the indignant voice of an enraged civilisation".[16] Soon afterwards it became possible for Baron Rothschild to take a seat in the House of Commons without taking an oath of loyalty to the Church of England—the law had been changed in 1858.

During the nineteenth century, the Russian Empire's five million Jews were, according to historian Orlando Figes, "at the bottom of its ethnic hierarchy ... subject to a comprehensive range of legal disabilities and discriminations".[17] Their linguistic and religious distinctiveness made them an easy target, and they had long been confined to the Pale of Settlement, the eastern parts of the huge Russian Empire. In her book *The Jews of South Wales*, Ursula Henriques suggests an explanation of why Jews were especially vulnerable. "There was a diaspora in every country of a people without a country, professing a religion repudiated

---

14 Dresser and Fleming, op cit, p93.
15 Annals of Bristol quoted by Judith Samuel in *Jews in Bristol* Redcliffe Press 1997.
16 *Bristol Mercury* 25 September 1858, quoted by Judith Samuel, op cit.
17 Orlando Figes *A People's Tragedy* Jonathan Cape 1996, p80.

by and repudiating the majority religions of their hosts, distinguished by its own languages—Hebrew and Yiddish or Ladino—bound by a detailed code of dietary laws and religious customs and sometimes dress, all calculated to prevent it dissolving into the societies in which it lived".[18] Their exclusion from land ownership and most craft guilds meant that many had to make a living by selling and by money lending, which made them unpopular at times of financial hardship.

When Czar Alexander was assassinated in 1881, Jews were widely though mistakenly blamed, and this led to a wave of pogroms. Then in 1886, Bismark expelled Jews from Prussia and the Board of Guardians for the Relief of the Jewish Poor in Britain responded in 1886 with "We beseech every right-thinking person among our brethren in Germany, Russia and Austria to place a barrier to the flow of foreigner".[19] Nevertheless, between 1881 and 1914 some 150,000 Jewish settlers moved to Britain. Some came to Bristol, and John Levy, a founding member of the Bristol Hebrew Literary and Debating Society, tried unsuccessfully to get Bristol's mayor to call a meeting about the plight of Russian Jews. Many were later to become active in the trade union movement in London, but at the time of what became known as the Great Depression (1873-1896), trade unions in Bristol were unsympathetic. In 1894, Christian Socialist and trade union activist H.H. Gore refused to employ a young female woman teacher on the grounds that she was Jewish.[20]

In 1905, the Conservative government passed the Aliens Act, an Act which could be invoked against any would-be immigrants to Britain—and was. "I have never been so ashamed of the House of Commons as I have been today", said Josiah Wedgewood MP.[21] Of Bristol's four MPs, only Charles Hobhouse, the Liberal member for Bristol East, spoke against the Act. Parliament passed further restrictions on 'alien immigration' in 1919 and 1920, and those restrictions were used to keep out Jews escaping from Nazi Germany in the 1930s. Those who managed to get to Bristol discovered that supporters of the Nazis—the British Union of Fascists—had a substantial base in the city. The BUF held meetings in Bedminster and at the Colston Hall, but both were disrupted. Oswald Mosley, the leader of the BUF, threatened his hecklers

---

18   Ursula Henriques *The Jews of South Wales* University of Wales Press 1993, p3.
19   Quoted by Robert Winder, op cit, p229.
20   Fleming and Dresser, p133. Mike Richardson *The Enigma of Hugh Holmes Gore* Bristol Radical History Group p109-113.
21   Quoted by Robert Winder, op cit, p259/60.

Colston in Bristol museum M Shed—now horizontal.

with "we will teach interrupters such a lesson that they will never come back to repeat their bad-mannered practices…".[22]

At the same time In Germany, a Jewish boy named Karl Hartland was discovering a change in attitude by his schoolteachers. A schoolboy prank—putting itching powder down the back of a school friend—led to his teacher telling him:

> For a boy in *your* situation, it is unwise to do anything that attracts special attention. You know there is a quota for young people and you are lucky to be here at all.[23]

It was the first step in the gradually increasing persecution that led eventually to him becoming one of the famous Kindertransport children. His mother had died young, but he vividly recalled the journey to the railway station with his father, and thinking the questions that he never asked: "Will I ever see you again?" and "Why are you staying behind?" Karl Hartland eventually became Charles Hannam, a much-loved lecturer in the education department of Bristol University. His father, like six million more Jews, died at the hands of the Nazis.

Vera Gissing, whose daughter lives in Bristol, recorded a vivid testimony of her experience as one of the Kindertransport.

Britain now seems inclined to pat itself on the back for enabling 669 Jewish children to escape from the Nazis in Czechoslovakia in 1938,

22 11 March 1936. Quoted by Rosemary L. Caldicott in *Lady Blackshirts* Bristol Radical History Group 2017, p22.
23 Charles Hannam *A Boy in Your Situation* Andre Deutsch 1977, p50 and p146/7.

and Nicholas Winton is rightly commended for his role in making that possible.[24] But the reason why those children travelled without their parents was because of the restrictive attitude of the UK government: "Britain's final gesture towards Germany's Jews before the outbreak of war was to hammer shut the exit routes by which they might have escaped".[25]

 Vira Gissing: Preparing for the Kindertransport

Black Bristol

If Jews in Bristol had a hard time of it, it was far worse for black people in the city, and very few found it a place of refuge. The notion that there was a slave market in Bristol, with 'Whiteladies' ascending 'Blackboy' Hill to buy slaves, is a total myth, but there were regular advertisements for runaway slaves in Bristol.[26] Some Africans in Bristol lived and died in slavery in the eighteenth century; although Scipio Africanus was honoured with an elaborate gravestone in Horfield, he had been a slave. In 2020 that gravestone was vandalised, apparently in response to the downing of the Colston statue.

The case of James Somerset in 1772 was of crucial importance. Judge Mansfield ruled that his 'master' had no right to compel him to board a ship. "Mansfield himself emphasised that he had not outlawed slavery but had merely ruled that slaves could not be forced to leave the country against their will".[27] So when Pero—only referred to by one name—arrived from St Nevis in Bristol in 1784, he would have known that at least one threat no longer hung over him.

Bristol has recently made much of Pero Jones, an enslaved African servant, naming a footbridge after him. "For many," write Mark Steeds and Roger Ball, "the fact that the bridge was not a dedicated memorial to the suffering of the enslaved, made the naming seem contrived and

---

24 *One Life* film directed by James Hawes, 2024.
25 Winder, op cit, p299.
26 Illustrated in Dresser and Fleming, op cit, p92.
27 Robert Winder, op cit, p126.

shallow: a last-minute gesture to placate critics".[28] A book about Pero Jones published in 2004 suggests that,

> ...given black servants were regarded as a status symbol and many West Indian planters, merchants and captains brought with them slaves and freed slaves, by Pero's time there must have been a sizable black population in Bristol...[29]

But even after the Mansfield judgement, the danger continued. In 1790, Hannah Moore reported the case of a black woman who had escaped from servitude in Bristol. "To my grief and indignation, the poor trembling wretch was dragged out from a hole in the top of a house where she had hid herself, and forced on board ship".[30] A year later Wilberforce attempted to persuade the House of Commons to pass a bill to end the slave trade. When his bill was defeated, there was a celebration on Brandon Hill and church bells rang out.[31] Welsh poet Iolo Morgannwg had just walked into the city and was so disgusted by the church's response that he turned around and left.[32]

It wasn't until 1807 that the slave trade was ended in Britain, and 1833 before the end of slavery in the British Empire. Even now much of the credit for the ending of a terrible crime is given to white abolitionists. "The notion that the enslaved people had played a role in their own emancipation," writes David Olusoga, "that liberty had been demanded and fought for, rather than simply given, was for the most part forgotten".[33]

Poles in Bristol

Just before the Second World War, Poland was the victim of both Nazi Germany and the Soviet Union, partitioned by both under the terms of the 1939 Nazi-Soviet Pact. Many Poles had to go through desperate adventures in order to get to Britain and so join the war against Nazi Germany.[34] Robert Winder in *Bloody Foreigners* describes them as heroes

28 Steeds and Ball, op cit, p269.
29 Christine Eickelmann and David Small *Pero* Redcliffe Press, p39.
30 Quoted by David Olusoga in *Black and British A Forgotten History* Macmillan, 2016, p103.
31 A footnote in *From Wulstan to Colston* records scepticism about the bell ringing.
32 Quoted by Prof Gwyn Alf Williams in Channel 4's *Bard of Liberty* transmitted 1997.
33 David Olusoga, op cit, p232.
34 Described by Stefan Petrusewicz on http://anglopolishsociety.org/podcast/stefan-petrusewicz/

Slave revolt in Barbados, 1823.

Polish guides marching in Bristol.

but also asserts that Poles could "also be noticeably and embarrassingly hostile to Jews".[35]

After the War, many of those who had fought alongside the British army were faced with a dilemma. Stanislaw Kucharczyk, who took part in the D Day invasion as part of the 1st Armour Division, recalled, "we were to return home. We all asked ourselves WHAT home? I knew that returning to Poland meant death or the Russian Siberian Camp." Eventually he found a shared house in Clifton, and a job. But,

> on my arrival on the first day at my new job, I found that all the workers at that factory went out on strike. The manager told me that I can't start my job because I was Polish and the workers resented this. The manager said that it was out of his hands and he could do nothing to help me. For a while I was stunned by their decision. I had tears in my eyes. What could I do now? How could I tell my family?[36]

35 Robert Winder, op cit, p321.
36 *In War and In Peace—Poles who came to the West Country* published by the Anglo Polish Society of Bristol and the South West, p113 and 119.

Robert Winder makes it clear that this shop floor response was not unique, though eventually the National Union of Mineworkers took a more sympathetic attitude. "By the end of 1948, 65,000 of the members of the Polish Resettlement Scheme had been placed in full employment … no one could deny that the scheme had been a success".[37] In 1968 the Polish community in Bristol bought Arley Chapel in Cheltenham Road from the Congregationalists and converted it into Our Lady of Ostrabrama church, adding Catholic wall engravings of the Fourteen Stations of the Cross in the process. When there are elections in Poland, it becomes a polling station and long queues spill out onto Cheltenham Road.

Asians in Bristol

"We are here, because you were there," said Sri Lankan writer Ambalavander Sivanadan.[38] This was true throughout the former British Empire but especially so for the Asians who came to Bristol as the Empire collapsed. Divide and rule, followed by the rushed decision to leave what became India and Pakistan, had terrible consequences, with massacres on both sides of the divide. The aftermath added to the number seeking sanctuary or work in the UK in the period after the Second World War. Many more came after partition and the continuing dispute over the ownership of Kashmir added to the number of emigrants. Others, predominantly people from Mirpur, were displaced by the building of the Mangla Dam.[39]

There was a second wave of Asian immigration after Idi Amin came to power in Uganda and launched an 'economic war' on the Asian community. In 1972, 27,000 Ugandan Asians headed for Britain. "It was traumatic and very hard to part with all our belongings our money and properties and leave empty handed", recalled Kantilal Rambhai and Sarlaben Kantilal Patel who eventually found a home in Bristol.[40] *Guardian* journalist Martin Walker wrote that Amin "became the saviour of the National Front, the best recruiting officer the National Front ever had".[41] Zehra Haq, who runs Dhek Bhal, a south Asian community organisation, recalls that in the Barton Hill area of Bristol,

37 Robert Winder, op cit, p324.
38 Quoted by Satnam Sanghera in *Empireland* Viking, 2021, p69.
39 Fleming and Dresser, op cit, p186.
40 Munwar Hussain (editor) *A Century of Migration* Bristol Library, 2006, p203.
41 Martin Walker *The National Front* Fontana Collins, 1977, p134.

Asian women "didn't feel comfortable because racism was very very rife at that time ... Even my Mother-in-Law had been attacked a few times ... yeah, she go to the park, she got hit, they pulled her scarf, the young kids, and they threw stones at her, so it was very frightening".[42]

The situation of Vietnamese refugees in the 1970s seemed to inspire more sympathy, with the *Daily Mail* becoming the unlikely initiator of a scheme for flying orphans out of Vietnam to safety in 1975. The fact that many Vietnamese fled from the Communist regime via sea routes, after the Americans were driven out, seemed to help to give them sympathetic media attention. Mai Van Thong escaped on a boat with more than 600 people on board:

> After two days we ran out of water and most of the people on the boat suffered from sea sickness ... But luckily a British sea captain realised our desperate situation ... we got to safety in the nick of time.[43]

Many of the Vietnamese in Bristol opened restaurants and take-aways, and Mai Van Thong became the project coordinator for a Vietnamese Refugee Centre in St Paul's.

As China tightened its grip on Hong Kong in 2021, more than 34,000 residents applied to come to the UK and 7,200 of these were swiftly approved. Some of the former activists who came to Bristol organised a protest demonstration against Chinese control here, but felt the kind of discomfort that is shared by many refugees in the city: "We are now safe, we are in a very good country ... but feel very guilty about leaving our friends and family and those protestors we fought with".[44]

Palestinians in Bristol have also continued their protest campaigns in the city, establishing a Palestine Museum and Cultural Centre in the city centre in 1973. Alissar was motivated by "the way the Palestinian cause has been manipulated. We are victims, we are condemned." Emad was surprised to come across the Museum: "it was a very good moment for me...I feel part of my home here".[45] There have been huge demonstrations in Bristol in support of the Palestinian cause and, in May 2024, Bristol University students set up a camp to protest at the

42 Quoted by Fleming and Dresser, op cit, p192.
43 Munwar Hussain, op cit.
44 thebristolcable.org/2021/08/escape-from-hong-kong-to-bristol/
45 palmuseumbristol.org/index/phk/video-gallery

Hong Kong protest in Bristol.

University's involvement, through research and financial investments, in companies profiting from the Israel-Hamas war.

Ali Zalme was from the town of Halabja in Iraq. Because those who lived there—and most of those who lived in northern Iraq—regarded themselves as Kurds, not as Iraqis, they were targeted with chemical weapons in 1988 and more than 5,000 were killed. "Small wonder that many Kurdish families and individuals emigrated" wrote Ali Zalme, who moved to Bristol and got a PhD at the University of the West of England on the Kurdish diaspora.[46] His research here eventually became the book *Home and a Sense of Belonging among Iraqi Kurds in the UK*. That 'sense of belonging' is what many immigrants in Bristol pine for.

Although this pamphlet has attempted to clarify the different experiences of immigrants in Bristol, it can be misleading to lump together the experiences of groups from very different nations. "It is by no means clear", writes Robert Winder, "…that we could find anything that looked like an 'Asian Community' in modern Britain, no matter how hard we tried … to herd them into just one bleak stockade marked 'Asian' would be to blur distinctions in the crudest way".[47] This would also be true of the label…

Africans in Bristol

In her novel *Black Mamba Boy* based on the experiences of her father's emigration to the UK, Nadifa Mohammed describes Somalia as "an afterthought of the empire builders, a small piece on a global monopoly board to be collected to spite the others".[48] Many Somali men had found work on British merchant ships but the numbers of Somali emigrants sharply increased when many sought to escape from the civil war of 1991. Mohammed Syeed had to take a bizarre way in order to get from Somalia to the UK, using the documentation of his sister Hafia. "I had a girl's dress, lipstick and some black stuff on my eyes. I had high heeled shoes, so I could not walk very well. I kept falling down … I had two apples under my jumper".[49]

Fleming and Dresser's detailed book on ethnic minorities in Bristol estimates that by 2007 there were some 20,000 Somalis in Bristol. They go on to highlight the fact that, although the 1976 Race Relations

46   Ali Zalme, article in *Bristol Globe* June 2012, p21.
47   Winder, op cit, p522.
48   Nadifa Mohammed *Black Mamba Boy* Harper, 2010, p78.
49   Geraldine Edwards coordinator *Origins* 1998, p72.

Act banned racial discrimination in public bodies, the Immigration Service was exempt. "Certainly racial harassment has been a frequent and widespread experience in Bristol", they write, "and this might be exacerbated by grouping Somalis together in highly concentrated and visible groups, without apparent regard for clan divisions".[50]

When Biniam Afawarq's father was arrested in Eritrea, he and his mother began the perilous journey to the UK. She disappeared on a raft that took them from Turkey to Greece, and he had to make it on his own to Calais, where he climbed on board a truck trailer than took him to England, eventually reaching Bristol. "I just wanted it to end—going from country to country, hiding from people, not having any food or money or a life".[51]

The 2011 census revealed that between 2001 and 2011 the British African population doubled, through both migration and natural increase. "For the first time, probably", commented David Olusoga, "since the age of the Atlantic slave trade, the majority of black Britons or their parents have come to this country directly from Africa, rather than somewhere in the Americas".[52] The experience of one of those migrants turns the statistics into what was all-too-often a painful personal experience. George Gumisiritza had to leave Uganda because of hostility from the regime that had earlier expelled its Asian citizens, eventually becoming a research student at Bristol University. "When migrants leave their countries of origin", he has written, "the loss is immense. Loss of self, culture, professions, possessions and family".[53]

Eastern Europe

The civil war that followed the collapse of what was Yugoslavia led to a substantial number of its former citizens seeking refuge in Bristol. Those who had been brought up in the Muslim faith were especially vulnerable to the 'ethnic cleansing' initiated by the Serbs who had once predominated. The war lasted from 1991 to 2001 and those who sought refuge in Britain were received sympathetically, in part because of the criticism of Serb aggression in media coverage of the civil war.

Those fleeing from Albania later got a markedly less sympathetic media response. After the collapse of Soviet-style communism that

50 Fleming and Dresser, op cit, p215.
51 Ellen Mauro report in *Bristol Globe* June 2013, p9.
52 David Olusoga, op cit, p524.
53 iwa.wales/agenda/2016/03/song-of-a-potted-plant

had followed the breaching of the Berlin Wall in 1989, Albania moved from a distortion of communism to a distortion of capitalism. "They had been promised 'democracy, markets and a constitutional order' by private industry organisations sent in by the American government but the reality", writes Lea Ypi, born and brought up in Albania but now living in Britian, "was increasing looting and violence in the streets and deteriorating economic conditions".[54] Newspapers like the *Daily Mail* slapped a criminal label on Albanians who sought refuge in Britain, but refugee organisations in Bristol soon became aware that many of those who came were family groups desperate for a better life. Those seeking refuge from Russia's invasion of Ukraine in 2014, which intensified in 2022, were regarded more sympathetically from the outset by the popular press in the UK.

It is impossible to tidy all immigrants to Bristol into neat geographical groups—even those who come from the same region of the same country are sometimes sharply divided by class, caste or political motivation. Some of those not previously mentioned came to Bristol because they felt they had to leave their own country—Hungarians after the 1956 rising, Czechs after the Russian invasion in 1968, and Chileans threatened by Pinochet's regime in 1973. Not migrating could have meant imprisonment or death, and that sense of a shared threat often bound political exiles together in their new city.

But even if some hoped one day to return to their own country, almost all came with the aim of securing a better life for themselves and their families—a motivation that is often given the dismissive label "economic migrants" with an implied unwelcoming response. Most of the new refugee and asylum seeker organisations that came into being in the 1970s refused to make any such distinction. If the new arrivals wanted help and support, the aim was to provide it.

Aid agencies and refugees

The International Red Cross had played a crucial role in enabling some Jewish children to get out of Czechoslovakia with the Kindertransport operation that Nicholas Winter had initiated. The scale of death and destruction during the Second World War was so colossal that attempts to alleviate it seemed puny, but it was the Red Cross that the Oxford Committee for Famine Relief turned to when it set out to respond to

54 Lea Ypi *Free—Coming of Age at the End of History* Penguin, 2022, p114.

the starvation in Greece in 1943. That Committee eventually grew into Oxfam and was one of the organisations that lobbied for the establishment of the international Refugee Convention in 1951. This asserted the right to claim asylum as an international human right, and the British government was one of the signatories to that Convention.

The Convention led to the formation of the British Council for Aid to Refugees and the Standing Conference on Refugees, later to combine to form the UK Refugee Council. While the Council was responding to the sympathy for refugees, others were articulating and generating hostility to all new arrivals in the UK. A virulently anti-immigrant candidate, Peter Griffiths, was elected as a Conservative MP for Smethwick in 1964, and during the 1970s members of the National Front began to get elected on to local councils in Bradford and Leicester (both cities with sizeable south Asian populations).

In 1979, just before she was elected as Prime Minister, Margaret Thatcher said in a television interview that "... people are really rather afraid that this country might by rather *swamped* by people with a different culture".[55] Her government's policies highlighted the need for campaigning organisations to defend refugees and asylum seekers. Refugee Action was started in 1981, initially to help to cope with the plight of the Vietnamese boat people. Soon after it established an office in Bristol and began a mentoring scheme in the city. New arrivals were paired with sympathetic Bristolians for a six-month period, and some of those links lasted for much longer.

Between 1996 and 2007, five laws were passed by the UK government restricting the rights of refugees and asylum seekers, and, in Bristol, organisations like Bristol Defend the Asylum Seekers began to emerge in opposition to those restrictions. Refugee Women of Bristol came into being in 2003, "aiming to raise the educational and economic status of refugee and asylum-seeking women."[56] Government support was limited, but that support was channelled through local authorities, so more locally based organisations emerged in response.

In 2004, psychotherapist Judy Ryde organised a conference in Bristol on "Holding Refugees in Mind". This led to a one day a week consultation for refugees and asylum seekers at Brookland Hall. It became clear that for many of them, recalled Naomi Roberts, "their right to remain was pending and their living conditions were awful".[57] They

---

55 Quoted by Caroline Elkins in *Legacy of Violence* Vintage 2023, p672.
56 refugeewomenofbristol.org
57 Conversation with the author.

A Bristol Refugee Rights logo, designed by Lizzie Wheeler.

were convinced that the urgent need was for a welcoming space, and this was initially provided at the Unitarian Church in Portland Square.

This initiative grew into the organisation Bristol Refugee Rights (BRR), set up as a voluntary organisation by Sue Njie in 2005, with Naomi Roberts and Dammy Le Grand as co-chairs. As the name of the new organisation suggests, there was an implicit criticism of the government's policies—an annual report recorded "a groundswell of concern about the asylum process" and made clear from the outset that it would "campaign for the rights of refugees and asylum seekers".[58] There was plenty to campaign about—in 2007 the government was to set up the UK Border Agency which gave immigration officers police powers to arrest and charge.[59]

Also in 2005, Ghanian-English singer-songwriter Lorraine Ayensu—from Bristol City Council Asylum services—organised a music event at the Hope Centre along with Tribe of Doris and refugee support agencies which eventually developed into the annual Celebrating Sanctuary event now held in Queen Square in the city centre.

From the outset Sue Njie argued for the need for community support for asylum seekers, and initially the Unitarian Church in Portland Square became a Welcome Centre. Successful funding applications soon enabled BRR to employ two members of staff, Caroline Beatty as Welcome Centre manager, and Sue Scott as the coordinator of the language programme entitled British Life and Language (BRILL). Eventually BRR, with funding help from Children in Need, was able to run a creche and an IT class, and to initiate the Bristol Bike Project, originally intended just for refugees and asylum seekers.

58 Bristol Refugee Rights Annual Report 2007-8, pp3 and 10.
59 Martin Spafford, Dan Lydon, Hakim Adi, Marika Sherwood *Migration* Hodder Education 2016, p120.

One of the very first refugees that BRR was able to help was Saman from Iran. His involvement in protests on behalf of fellow Kurds had led to the Iranian police putting a noose around his neck with a warning that next time it would be for real. He got to Bristol by hiding in a lorry and, after a period of depression, BRR had helped him back on his feet.[60] After setting up a successful food shop, he now runs the thriving Sam Master Grill in Cheltenham Road.

The BRR report for 2007-8 recorded that "75% of asylum claimants are refused asylum here—they all face destitution" and Rachel Bee, an energetic BRR staff member, responded by creating the Bristol Hospitality Network (BHN) in 2009, generously enabling her own house to be used to accommodate new arrivals in Bristol. Later BHN was donated a house for the project. Elinor Harris, its advice manager, says that "it filled a huge gap in services for asylum seekers in Bristol" stressing that it is always coordinating with other support groups "to ensure we don't duplicate".[61]

Borderlands was set up by Father Richard MacKay in the Assisi Centre in 2011 alongside the Catholic Church of St Nicholas of Tolentino. This made some Muslim refugees and asylum seekers wary of the charity, but its website—and its practice—stresses that "we work with people regardless of race, disability, sex, age, religious belief or sexual orientation".[62] Following the example of Sheffield City Council, a number of Bristol refugee and asylum seekers pressed for the city to become a City of Sanctuary, and on 2nd June 2011 the City Council passed the motion that "recognises the contribution of asylum seekers and refugees to the City of Bristol and is committed to welcome and including them in our activities."

Hostility to refugees and asylum seekers

Some letters to the local press made clear that not everyone in the city was inclined to be welcoming. Robert Readman wrote to the *Western Daily Press* in 2011 attacking the Chair of the Equality and Human Rights Commission: "Does he really believe that extreme Muslims who scream abuse at our brave soldiers, branding them murderers, are seeking integration into our society?"[63] David Challice of the UK

---

60 Conversation with author 26 February 2024.
61 bhn.org.uk/our-story
62 borderlands.uk.com/whoweare
63 *Western Daily Press* 23 June 2011.

Independence Party claimed in the same newspaper that the "floodgates opened for asylum seekers", going on to argue that the European Court "has now stripped Britain of the right to deport asylum seekers to other EU countries.[64]

The most damning evidence of unsympathetic attitudes to refugees by some in Bristol emerged in the case of Bijam Ebrahimi. Bijam was a disabled refugee who had been imprisoned and tortured in Iran. His neighbours in Brislington wrongly accused him of being a paedophile and police ignored his pleas for help. Vigilante attacks on him culminated in his murder on 14th July 2013, when he was stabbed to death and his body set on fire. There is a sad visual memorial to him in the entrance to Bristol City Hall which says "Sorry" in different languages. After a damning report by the Independent Commission on Police Conduct,[65] two of the officers who had failed to respond to Bijam's pleas for protection were sent to prison for misconduct. The police were also sharply criticised in the case of Kamil Ahmad, an asylum seeker, who was murdered in a Bristol hostel by a paranoid schizophrenic in 2016 with whom he had been accommodated.

In October 2013 Mark Harper, the Conservative MP for the Forest of Dean, who initiated the Home Office's 'Go Home' ads on vans, used a live BBC Bristol studio discussion with Iraqi Kurdish refugee Esam Amin in October 2013 to make a virulent attack on him. "I am not an illegal person", insisted Esam, "I am a human being like you. My life in my country is in danger". "You have no right to be in the UK", retorted Harper, "you should leave".[66] Five years later Esam was given leave to remain.

Finding a voice

"We became extremely concerned about the way in which these issues were being handled in the media", wrote Mike Jempson, who taught journalism at the University of the West of England. "Truth, fairness and balance were giving way to myth, speculation and bigotry".[67] Mike became the director of MediaWise, and the Refugees, Asylum-

64 *Western Daily Press* 28 June 2011.
65 https://www.policeconduct.gov.uk/sites/default/files/documents/December_2022_Disclosure_Log.pdf
66 dailymail.co.uk/news/article-2458617/Mark-Harper-tells-time-failed-asylum seeker-home-live-TV.html
67 https://www.media-diversity.org/additional-files/documents/b-studies-reports/The%20RAM%20Report%20%5BEN%5D.pdf

seekers and the Media Project (RAM) he founded set out to ensure that refugees and asylum-seekers obtained fair and accurate representation in the media. By 2005, the RAM report could report positively on Bristol Defend the Asylum-seekers' campaign work with the local media, particularly, said the report, the *Bristol Evening Post*. It had also effectively challenged outrageous misreporting in national newspapers like *The Sun* who had invented a bizarre story about refugees murdering swans. In June 2011, the *Bristol Globe* magazine was launched, "offering a warm welcome to those who come and live here, and a reminder to the rest of us about where we come from and what we can offer each other".[68] Its June 2012 edition was able to celebrate the official launch of Bristol as a City of Sanctuary.

The *Bristol Cable* newspaper has also consistently provided a more sympathetic perspective to the city's immigrants. In 2014 on 21st March, the Kurdish national day, some Kurdish refugees provided an insight into their fractured identity. "You're divided in between two lives", said Ali, a PhD student at UWE; "this affects every moment of your life. We come from a suspended state. We are always divided by two places".[69]

This was also true for Bnar who grew up in the Kurdish controlled area of Iraq. A successful photojournalist working for Iraqi magazines, she sometimes found it difficult working with religious restraints at home and moved to the UK. After coping with a disturbed night at Reading railway station and then a frightening night at a Bristol hostel, support from Bristol Refugee Rights enabled her to convince the Home Office and so to get leave to remain with comparative speed.[70] She is now completing a course on photojournalism at Cardiff University, and her project on Yemeni women in Cardiff was selected for exhibition at the National Portrait Gallery.

By 2014, Bristol Refugee Rights was involved in two initiatives designed to help refugee and asylum seekers find expression: the VOICE project focussed on volunteering and community engagement; and Pride Without Borders which focussed on newcomers who were LGBTQ refugees, helping them to find their feet in the UK. In over 80 countries it is a crime or extremely unsafe to be LGBTQ. The VOICE project, which was set up with the City of Bristol College and managed by Qerim Nuredin, included training in public speaking. "Because of your skin tone", wrote Nikesh Shukula, "they'll ask where your parents are from.

68   Mike Jempson editorial *Bristol Globe* June 2011, p4.
69   thebristolcable.org/2014/10/Kurdish-debate
70   Conversation with the author, 26 March 2024.

Ken Macharia—local
protests saved him
from deportation.

If you tell them Bristol, they'll ask [you] where your parents are from."
His response was to edit 21 essays by black, Asian and minority ethnic
voices, and publish it in 2016 under the title *The Good Immigrant*.[71] It
spelt out the difficulty of moving from what "The Ungrateful Country"
deems a 'bad' immigrant to becoming a 'good' one.

Ken Macharia achieved that transition. Involved in both VOICE and
Pride Without Borders, he was a mechanical engineer with a secure job.
He was also a popular member of the Bristol Bisons, an inclusive team
that was part of the Gay Rugby League. But in 2018 he was detained in
order for him to be expelled to Kenya, despite that country's notorious
hostility to its gay citizens—gay relationships had been criminalised by
the Kenyan government and this decision was later upheld by its High
Court.

"My confidence was at the lowest when I was locked up in a detention
centre", he later recalled, "I was feeling extremely hopeless".[72] But fellow
members of the Bristol Bisons rallied round and launched a petition
that soon had thousands of signatures. He was eventually released from
detention, and in 2021 won his appeal. Ken is now one of the trustees of
Bristol Refugee Rights.

71 Nikesh Shukla editor *The Good Immigrant* Unbound, 2016, p1. *The Ungrateful Country* essay
by Musa Okwonga, p224.
72 https://exhibitions.bristolmuseums.org.uk/crossings-community-refuge/ken/

Sherien Elsheikh, who came originally from war-torn Libya, also experienced the worst and best of Bristol:

> I went out without my husband and was pushing my little baby on his pushchair. Some teenagers attacked me, using bad words and throwing stones. There is no language, no protection, I cannot describe that feeling. I wanted to cry so badly … I felt unwanted.

But later: "I also had the good fortune to feel a sense of welcome. I have worked a lot in volunteer work … meeting people with joy is a sign of welcome".[73]

Aid Box in Bristol developed out of their work in Calais in 2015 and now runs a free shop and welcome hub in the city. Charities have to be careful about how critical they can be without losing their charitable status, but Aid Box's website doesn't pull its punches:

> Those who are not granted asylum face destitution and deportation and are often held in deportation centres—some for years. Some granted asylum end up homeless and destitute due to lack of mental health, employment and housing support.[74]

All the Bristol organisations which aim to help refugee and asylum seekers face the frustration of the absence of a legal method of claiming asylum from outside the UK.

The Bristol Refugee Festival began in 2017. Like most of the organisations in Bristol that were set up to help refugee and asylum seekers, it aimed to involve them in the process, working *with* them rather than on their behalf. So, when Refugee Action set up an office in Bristol, it appointed as its deputy manager Qerim Nuredini who had left Kosovo during the brutal civil war that followed the collapse of Yugoslavia. Similarly, Mohammed Osman, who soon moved from being a refugee to helping other refugees at Refugee Action, is now the Migration Inclusion Strategic Lead on Bristol City Council. He had once suffered beatings by the French police at the notorious camp at Calais, before climbing on to the back of a lorry to get to the UK. "I have first-hand experience about the system, and the barriers surrounding

---

73 Bristol Refugee Festival blog 2024.
74 aidboxcommunity.co.uk/ourstory

Bristol Refugee Festival in Queen Square.

the needs of refugees and asylum seekers", he has written; "This has given me insights into the challenges and barriers asylum seekers and refugees will be facing".[75]

In 2019, Bristol Refugee and Asylum Seeker Partnership (BRASP) was created within the refugee and asylum seeker (RAS) support sector between fifteen Bristol-based organisations, including those already mentioned together with Trauma Foundation South West, Ashley Community Housing, Project Mane, The Haven and Bristol Reporting Solidarity.

The plight of refugees from the Russian invasion of Ukraine attracted more government sympathy than those fleeing from other war zones and, since 2022, Bristol has accommodated over 800 Ukrainian refugees, overwhelmingly women and children, through the Homes for Ukraine scheme. Very few of those have come through Bristol Refugee Rights, but that organisation enables those who do use its services to become members; it stresses that it is a member-led organisation and holds regular meetings at which members can put over their points of view. One of those members, Nabil, a Kurdish artist from Iraq,

75 linkedin.com/in/mohammed-osman-024609a4

eloquently expressed what involvement meant to him: "Before I worked with those charities, I was like a bird without wings. They gave me the wings to fly to help the people".[76]

 Voice of America Unpacked: Life as a Refugee

Refugees and migrants—gains and losses

Suketu Mehta writes bluntly:

> If the rich countries *don't* want the poor countries to migrate then there's another solution. Pay them what they're owed. Pay the costs of colonialism, of the wars imposed on them, of the inequality you've built into the world order, and the carbon you've out into the atmosphere.[77]

Industrialised countries deliberately started most of the major international flows of migrants of the past century, but some commentators steer clear of Mehta's approach, preferring to spell out the positive advantages that immigrants bring: they "often create more jobs than they take, are likely to pay more in taxes than they use in welfare, and far from undermining settled nations these new arrivals constantly enrich and fortify the multicultural societies they enter".[78]

That enrichment is displayed every year in the Bristol Refugee Festival. Lorraine Ayensu died tragically young of a brain tumour in 2012, but her memory is kept alive through Lorraine Ayensu Refugee Arts (LARA) which helps to arrange the music events at the festival.

Paul Collier in his book, *EXODUS—How Migration Is Changing the World*, takes a gloomy view of the impact of recent immigration. He points out the cost to the countries that are losing some of the brightest and best of their citizens and continues:

76 Bristol Refugee Festival blog.
77 Suketu Mehta *This Land Is Our Land—An Immigrant's Manifesto* Vintage, 2019, p192.
78 Peter Stalker *The No-Nonsense Guide to International Migration* New Internationalist/Verso, 2001, p9.

The massive productivity gains from migration that so excite economists and that migrants capture appear not to translate into additional well-being ... In the worst-case scenario, continuing psychological costs would offset the gains for several generations; migration would not be an investment, it would be a mistake.[79]

Later Collier acknowledges the link between climate change and migration and writes: "the weakening of mutual regard is the more important danger on which to focus because it is less obvious and probably has long lags".[80] What is striking about Bristol's response to immigration is that, so far, there has been little sign of that weakening of mutual regard. "Our vision", concludes Tom Daly and Kate Evans's booklet on the UK asylum process, "is a society where refugees, asylum seekers and migrants are welcomed, feel safe, live free of poverty and are able to positively build their lives".[81]

79 Paul Collier *EXODUS—How Migration Is Changing Our World* Oxford University Press, 2015, p176.
80 Ibid, p258.
81 Tom Daly and Kate Evans *Escape to Safelandia* Research and Knowledge Exchange, Aston University and Research England, p80.

Suggested reading

Robert Winder, *Bloody Foreigners* (Abacus, 2005)

Kate Evans and Tom Daly, *Escape to Safelandia* (https://www.cartoonkate.co.uk/escape-to-safelandia/)

Paul Collier, Exodus—How migration is changing the world (OUP, 2013)

Peter Stalker, *The No-Nonsense Guide to International Migration* (Verso, 2001)

Sathnam Sanghera, *Empireland* (Viking, 2021)

Acknowledgements

The author wishes to express his gratitude for helpful advice he received from Kitty Odell, Naomi Roberts, Dammy Le Grand, Silu Pascoe, Andrew McCarthy, Mike Jempson, Ken Macharia, Qerim Nuredini, Mohammed Osman, George Gumisiriza, Saman, Bnar and the refugees and asylum seekers who cannot be identified because they or their relatives are at risk from their own governments or from that of the U.K. Especial thanks to Richard Musgrove for his patient and perceptive editing of this publication and for the advice of its Bristol Radical History Group readers. The author takes responsibility for any errors.

Picture Credits

Front cover—Tristan Cork, *Bristol Post*.

Page 5—"The Huguenots in England: French Huguenot refugees landing at Dover in 1685 after the Revocation of the Edict of Nantes." *The Graphic*, 24 October 1885.

Page 7—John Rocque's map of Bristol, 1742, engraved by John Pine, published by Benjamin Hickey, 1743.

Page 10—Bristol City Council.

Page 13—*Account of an insurrection of the negro slaves in the colony of Demerara, which broke out on the 18th of August, 1823*, Joshua Bryant, Publiched by A. Stevenson At the Guiana Chronicle Office, Georgetown.

Page 14—Bristol Anglo-Polish Society.

Page 17—Bristol HK Campaign Group.

Page 22—Courtesy Lizzie Wheeler & Bristol Refugee Rights.

Page 26—Courtesy Ken Macharia.

Page 28—Bristol Archives 46261/4/5.

Inside back cover—*Escape to Safelandia* by Kate Evans and Tom Daly.

ESCAPE TO SAFELANDIA

A CHOOSE-YOUR-MISADVENTURE COMIC ABOUT THE UK ASYLUM SYSTEM

This is a comic about the asylum process here in the UK, the British history of welcoming refugees, and recent legislation which makes it harder to provide humanitarian assistance to people in need.   CONTENT WARNING: contains references to sexual assault, forced marriage, child slavery, gun crime, human rights abuses and the UK asylum system.

KATE EVANS AND TOM DALY

Bristol has been host to refugees for centuries—but just how welcoming has the city been?

The events of the first week of August 2024 follow a pattern that stretches back centuries—refugees and asylum seekers seeking refuge in Bristol and encountering hostility from some, but a welcome from others.

Colin Thomas's short history charts the reception given to those fleeing war and persecution from the seventeenth century to the twenty-first, outlines the stories of organisations that have developed to support these refugees in Bristol and, finally, poses some difficult questions we have to ask.

£3

ISBN 978-1-911522-

9 781911 522782